Living in the World of a Child

LUKE MENSAH AKROSUMA

Published by LUKE MENSAH AKROSUMA, 2023.

While every precaution has been taken in the preparation of this book, the publisher assumes no responsibility for errors or omissions, or for damages resulting from the use of the information contained herein.

LIVING IN THE WORLD OF A CHILD

First edition. June 25, 2023.

Copyright © 2023 LUKE MENSAH AKROSUMA.

ISBN: 979-8223775133

Written by LUKE MENSAH AKROSUMA.

Table of Contents

To all parties in the parenting process.

LIVING IN THE WORLD OF A CHILD

A MUST READ FOR ALL PARENTS

ACKNOWLEDGEMENT

The greatest of the gratitude goes to the Creator of the universe. The penultimate appreciation goes to my parents, through whom I experienced a type of parenting.

Lastly to all and sundry, I say may the Creator replenish all your loss.

DEDICATION

This book is dedicated to all parties in the parenting process

INTRODUCTION

Parenting is a process that evolves from child birth through to child upbringing. In other words, parenting involves mothering and fathering a child. In addition, parenting also captures warding another person usually, a younger one by an elderly. Parenting is a determinant of the child's perception of the world s/he finds himself/herself.

The parenting process that involves two main actors; the parent and the ward.

These two actors have their onus in the parenting process. The parent is required to establish an environment needed to catalyze the growth of the child. The latter must be willing and ready to go through the process of being warded. Thus, for a successful parenting process, there must be in existence a congenial relation between the two parties.

Many a time, this prerequisite atmosphere is non-existent between the aforementioned parties owing to the style adopted by parents. These disconnects result to gaps in the developmental process.

The impact and repercussion of this disconnect coupled with the antidote is discussed in this book.

CHAPTER ONE

PARENTING STYLES

A parent's manner of behavior and approach to raising their child can be characterized as their parenting style. Parenting styles differ from specific child-rearing approaches because they provide comprehensive models of behaviors and conduct that create an emotional environment for the child. Parenting approaches also reflect how parents interact with their kids and place expectations on them. The assumption underlying the examination of parenting styles is that parents have different parenting models, and that these models can have a big impact on the development and wellbeing of their kids.

Developmental psychologists make a distinction between the parent-child relationship, which is ideally one of attachment, and the parent-child relationship, referred to as bonding. Parents face new obstacles throughout the adolescent stage since teenagers are more independent and want more freedom. Children go through many stages in life, and parents establish their own parenting philosophies based on a variety of elements that change over time as kids start to come into their own as individuals. Parents attempt to adapt to a new lifestyle while their child is in the infancy period in order to bond with and bond with their new baby.

The parenting style a child may experience depends on their temperament and their parents' cultural norms. The parenting philosophies adopted by parents are also influenced by how they were reared.

The responsiveness, democracy, emotional involvement, control, acceptance, dominance, and restrictiveness of parenting styles were all topics of early research. Diana Baumrind developed a taxonomy of three parenting philosophies in the 1960s and classified them as authoritarian, permissive, and authoritative (or indulgent). She defined the authoritative style as the best compromise between control and autonomy. This typology evolved into the prevalent classification of parenting approaches, frequently with the addition of a fourth group for parents who are uncaring or neglectful.

Some early researchers found that children raised in a democratic home environment were more likely to be aggressive and exhibit leadership skills while those raised in a controlled environment were more likely to be quiet and non-resistant. Contemporary researchers have emphasized that love and nurturing children with care and affection encourages positive physical and mental progress in children. They have also argued that additional developmental skills result from positive parenting styles, including maintaining a close relationship with others, being self-reliant, and being independent.

In this book, we shall situate our discussions on four parenting styles. These are;

Authoritarian Parenting: Authoritative Parenting: Permissive Parenting and Uninvolved Parenting.

Authoritarian Parenting

Parents that are strict feel that children should always abide by the rules.

When a child queries the justification for a regulation, authoritarian parents are infamous for replying, " I said this," They are more concerned with obeying than they are with bargaining. Additionally, they forbid kids from participating in hurdles or challenges that require problem-solving. Instead, they establish the guidelines and administer the sanctions with little consideration for a child's viewpoint.

Additionally, they might turn hostile or violent. They frequently concentrate on the rage they feel against their parents or themselves for not living up to parental expectations rather than how to do things better in the future. Since authoritarian parents are frequently strict, their kids may develop into skilled liars as a result.

In a nut shell, the authoritarian is characterized by the following stance.

- What the child feels is irrelevant.
- The child has nothing to say. S/he must be a listener.
- My decision is final.

Parental authority figures may substitute punishment for instruction. Therefore, they are interested in making youngsters feel bad about their mistakes rather than teaching them how to make better decisions. When their parents are stern and authoritarian, children have a tendency to follow the rules most of the time. But there is a cost to their compliance.

Due to their lack of respect, children of authoritarian parents are more likely to experience issues with their self-esteem.

Authoritative Parenting

Parents who are authoritative enforce rules and impose penalties, but they also consider their children's viewpoints. They acknowledge their children's emotions while simultaneously emphasizing that the adults are in charge in the end. This method is supported by science and professionals as the most productive and developmentally sound parenting style.

Parents who are authoritative put time and effort into avoiding behavioral issues before they arise. Additionally, they employ positive discipline techniques like reward and praise systems to reinforce good conduct.

Researchers have found kids who have authoritative parents are most likely to become responsible adults who feel comfortable self-advocating and expressing their opinions and feelings

Children who are disciplined with authority are more likely to be content and successful. They are also more likely to be competent independent decision-makers and risk assessors of safety.

The Authoritative parent believes in the following factors in parenting.

- Giving reasons for every rule
- establishing and preserving a good relationship with your child.
- Set boundaries, uphold regulations, and administer penalties while keeping in mind your child's feelings.

Permissive Parenting

They have a very tolerant mindset and embrace children as they are. When they do apply penalties, they might not make those penalties last. If a youngster begs for their privileges, they might return them, and if they promise to behave well, they might let them out of time-out early.

Parents that are liberal with their children typically act more like friends than parents. They frequently encourage their kids to talk to them about their issues, but they typically don't make an attempt to prevent wrong decisions or bad behavior.

Children who have lenient parents are more likely to have academic difficulties as adults.

Because they don't respect authority and norms, they could have greater behavioral issues. They frequently exhibit low self-esteem and may express great melancholy.

Additionally, they are more susceptible to health issues like obesity since permissive parents find it difficult to encourage regular exercise, healthy eating, or good sleep hygiene. Because lax parents frequently don't enforce beneficial behaviors, including making sure a child brushes their teeth, they are significantly more likely to have dental cavities.

The permissive parent is characterized by these parental approaches.

- Believing the child will learn on his/her own
- Barely enforcing set rules.
- Reluctant to issue punishment for offences

They frequently don't intervene until a significant issue arises.

Uninvolved Parenting

Parents who aren't involved often, don't know much about what their kids are up to. There are typically not many rules in the home. There may not be enough parental guidance, care, and attention for the kids.

Parents who aren't involved expect their kids to raise themselves. They don't put much effort or time into providing for the basic necessities of children. Even though neglect by absent parents might occur, it's not always on purpose. For instance, a parent struggling with mental health concerns or substance abuse disorders might not be able to consistently meet a child's physical or emotional requirements. Here,

- Your youngster is not questioned about their studies or assignments.
- Rarely do you know where or with whom your child is.
- Your child and you don't spend much time together.

CHAPTER TWO

13

SEX LIFE OF YOUR CHILD

The subject of sex happens to be one of the most ignored when it comes to issues of discourse in parenting.

The concept of Sex

In one breadth sex refers to all behaviors that can arouse your sexual desire. Penetrative sex (sex that penetrates) is only one aspect of sex. It also covers acts like kissing, cuddling, finger playing, and oral sex. Having sex with oneself is another option. The term for this is masturbation. An additional aspect of sex is a group of biological characteristics present in both humans and animals. Physiological characteristics, such as chromosomes, gene expression, hormone levels and functions, and reproductive/sexual anatomy are primarily involved. Although sex is typically classified as either female or male, there are differences in the biological characteristics that make up sex and how those characteristics are exhibited.

Our discussions in this chapter shall however place emphasis on the former aspect of sex in the life of children. There comes a time in child's life where the physiological make-up of the child places demands to be satisfied. It's crucial to comprehend how kids' sexual development progresses as they get older. The environment, experiences, and things children witness have an impact on how they develop sexually. Compared to their parents, children today are more likely to see or come across sexually explicit photos and videos at a younger age. This can be done via movies, music videos, or online content like porn.

The interest in relationships, sex, and sexuality can develop at somewhat different ages for every child because they are all unique. However, as kids grow older, so are the ways in which they communicate their sexual desires. Teenagers' interest in sex and relationships, for instance, or children's curiosity about changes that occur throughout puberty, are both common occurrences.

As long as they don't endanger themselves or others, many sexual behaviors that children and teenagers exhibit as they mature are acceptable and healthy.

Knowing whether their child's sexual behavior is becoming inappropriate or dangerous can be quite difficult for parents. A child's words regarding sexual behavior may cause you to become concerned, or you may notice sexualized behavior between your child and a buddy or peer.

Children and teenagers occasionally exhibit sexual behavior that is out of character for their age group. For teenagers, growing up and going through changes like puberty can be challenging and emotionally taxing. Some young toddlers may make awkward efforts at sexual behavior that distress others.

Reasons for engaging in sex-general

It is important to note that the major purposes for sex revolves around procreation, experiencing intimacy and pleasure, expressing love and other emotions. Considering the aforementioned reasons, can we say a developing child will have reason to indulge in sex and its related activities? It is worthy to remind ourselves as already mentioned, sex involves but not limited to the following; kissing: cuddling: finger playing: oral sex and masturbation.

Reasons for which a growing child will have sex

Thus, an adolescent child might find reasons like those enlisted below to indulge in sex and its related activities.

- Experiencing intimacy and pleasure
- Experiencing love (infatuation) and other emotion
- Quest to satisfy burning desire
- Quest to gratify curiosity
- Quest to realize fantasies.

Its factually admissible that every growing child goes through all these physiological changes though at distinct time periods. Knowledge of these aspect of the child's life would facilitate successful parenting.

Child readiness for sex and sex related pursuits

Depending on the type of parenting style adopted, the following are highly probable symptomatic occurrences in the child's sex life the parent should take note of.

- Child beginning to be extremely cautious about what to wear at a given time. The child at this point has peculiar taste for how s/he looks in a particular attire. At this stage, the appearance is of prime importance to his or her development. They pick and choose what to wear. Their goal is to look appealing to the outside world through the tone of their clothing. At this stage, the statement: dress as you want to be addressed becomes largely evident. The authoritative parent is ideal to spot this symptomatic development in time to provide the necessary assistance.

- The child becomes more concerned about the manner they are spoken to in public. They attach keen importance to the manner they are addressed. At the stage the child feels awful when communicated to disrespectfully. They tend to dislike those who give no recourse to their feelings by talking to them anyhow. Respect is reciprocal becomes the order of the day. Here, the child is also watchful with the choice of words uttered. Owing to the lackadaisical nature of the permissive and uninvolving parents, hardly would they have a smooth interaction with their children.

- The growing child tend to be attracted to certain class of people. S/he builds up personal reasons find a person attractive or repulsive. Identity of such individuals in many instances are kept private and unknown to the parents of the developing child with particular reference to the type of parenting style employed. The authoritative parent is however more likely placed to identify to get informed about this special person or group of persons in the child's life. The permissive and uninvolving parent may get to know but might not give it the needed attention and reaction. However, the authoritarian parent might not get to know of this phenomenon about the child owing to the communication gap that exist between the two parties.

CHAPTER THREE

THE LOVE OF YOUR CHILD

Humanity exists for the sake of love; the essence of humanity is humanitarian. Others believe love is what sustains the world. Many of the provision made by parents for children is grounded on love.

The concept of Love

In one angle (noun) love can be described as an intense feeling of deep affection: a great interest and pleasure in something or a person or thing that one loves.

In another perspective, to love is to feel deep affection for (someone): to like an entity in a great deal.

For the purpose of our discussions, we shall view love as a deep feeling of affection, attraction which causes selfless commitment towards the one been loved. In other words, love is a collection of emotions and actions marked by intimacy, passion, and commitment. It involves care, closeness, protectiveness, attraction, affection, and trust. Love can vary in intensity and can change through time. Its worthy to note that, love is bilateral involving two parties: the one showing the love and the one receiving the love.

Types of love

- **Liking**. You have a close emotional bond, but there is little physical ardor or dedication. This category includes friendship.
- **Infatuation**. Infatuation's essential ingredient is passion. Infatuation is when you are physically attracted to someone but have not yet established emotional connection or a commitment.
- **Empty**. A committed relationship devoid of passion or intimacy is referred to as "empty love" by Sternberg. Examples include an arranged marriage or a once-intense romantic or sexual connection that has fizzled out.
- **Romantic**. When you're romantically linked with someone, you experience intense physical attraction and close emotional connection, but you haven't committed to anything long-term.
- **Companionate**. You are emotionally linked and dedicated, such as with close friends or relatives. If the desire is gone but you still share the commitment and emotional tie, marriages can still be companionate.
- **Fatuous**. This is fanciful love if you've been carried up in passion into an engagement or marriage without emotional intimacy.
- **Consummate**. Many people who picture marriage or a marital partnership aim for complete love. This form of love entails dedication, ardor, and close emotional ties.

Various forms of love exist. You can love multiple people at once and in various ways. Not all partnerships involve emotional closeness, but many do. The same is true of commitment and enthusiasm. Another aspect of a relationship that may be present in love is attachment. Positive relationships give you emotional support and a sense of security.

Why would a developing child practice love?

- **To show care**. In love transaction, the one showing the love tends to show care to the one receiving the care. Love tends to always profess one of the parties as weak whereas the other is understood to be resilient. The growing child would have entities s/he cares about and those that s/he expects care from. There could also be a reciprocal trade for care too.

- **For pleasure and happiness**. Some aspect of love seeks to ensure that the parties happiness and pleasure is met by amplifying efforts aimed at realizing this goal. The developing child shall obviously have sources for happiness and pleasure. As a parent, it would be very crucial to get to know of your child source of happiness to offer the necessary buffer.

- **To satisfy sexual desires**. The sexual emotions stemming from human desires plays a pivotal role in love. Parties involved work at realizing this aspect of love. The onset of adolescence causes the growing child to undergo some physiological changes including the need to honor their sexual cravings. These cravings if not tamed might be over-exploited. The adverse effects of this act might outweigh the positives. Parents must be on the lookout for this phenomenon.

- **To have a positive self-esteem by being valued**. Love makes one feel accepted; it prevents one from feeling sidelined and deserted. The growing child shall feel the need to belong to a certain group of people. Thus, they expect to be be accepted and treated as people of worth.

- **To show commitment**. Some believe love is sacred. Thus, to show true love, commitment must be evidently characterized. At this stage, they tend to show commitment by giving out some of their items to individuals they think might be in dire need of such items. Thus, they give out to people or entities they care about or think about. This act is intended to sustain a relationship they might have started or want to start.

Child readiness to practice love.

- The child begins to have specific groups of people s/he is nice to. They often get excited around such people.
- Expresses a feeling of safety around certain group of people.
- Begins to regularly speak well about a person or group of persons.
- Becomes fond of particular person or group of people.
- Shares whatever s/he gets with a certain group of people or person.

CHAPTER FOUR

THE STRENGTHS OF YOUR CHILD

Knowledge of the strength of your child is crucial in guiding him/her towards achieving the future aspirations envisaged.

The concept of strength.

Tasks or acts you excel at are considered strengths. Knowledge, proficiency, skills, and talents fall under this category. People use their characteristics and skills to carry out tasks, interact with others, and accomplish goals. Strengths are admirable qualities that highlight a person's skills, talents, or personality traits and can offer them an advantage over others or help them achieve a goal.

Types of strength.

- **Personal strength:** Our innate abilities meant for distinct ways of thinking, feeling, and acting are known as personal strengths. Personal strengths are qualities, pursuits, or tasks in which you thrive. Consider personality attributes like charisma, sociability, or open-mindedness as examples. These strengths are catalyst for personal growth of the child.

- **Professional strength:** They often consist of a combination of hard and soft talents as well as knowledge you've gained from your professional life. Simply put, you are good at a particular job because of your professional abilities. Here, each person will have a distinctive combination of professional abilities, and thus those who can sell their experiences to employers most persuasively will succeed. These include special skill sets employed in the performance of an assigned task.

Identifying the strength of your child.

The growing child exhibits qualities that describe his/her personality. These qualities are usually employed in the discharge of assigned task and way of life in general. The following must keenly be noted to identify the strength of a child.

- What your child likes doing every day. The personal daily routine of a child defines his/her choices of fondness. These activities express what the child is comfortable at doing. Naturally, no one will find affinity in doing what s/he detests. A child may enjoy playing football every day. As an art backed by science, practice will surely increase his or her abilities in playing. This also applies to other activities like reading: dancing and other things the child might find worthy of spending time on.
- What the child regularly talks about given certain time frame. Naturally, everyone will like to talk about what s/he is more at ease with. The content of their conversation sends a signal about their preference and perception about things.
- What mistake the child keeps making. In their daily assigned tasks, a critical observation shall reveal tasks that children perform with some degree of discomfort. Repetitive difficulties observed communicates a child trying to make a strength out of a weakness.

CHAPTER FIVE

34

THE WEAKNESS OF YOUR CHILD

As we live in an interactive world, the need to carry out certain duties shall always be a part of us. In the execution of our assigned task, discomfort do prevail indicating our lower knowledge or ability demanded in the performances of the task in question.

The concept of weakness.

The attribute or state of weakness is that lacks vigor, firmness, strength, or success. Weakness describes the fact or state of not being strong or powerful. It may refer to a feeble condition or state. It can also be used to describe a drawback or blunder. A difficulty in dealing with a situation does not fully constitute weakness rather, the consistent intimation of difficulty in the performance of an activity is what constitute weakness.

Causes of weakness

Human development evolves around interaction with the outside world coupled with the performance of certain tasks be it mandatory or voluntary. However, owing to certain factors, developing children are unable to perform or interact as expected. Among such reasons are the following;

- Inadequate knowledge about the task at hand.
- Inadequate experience about the task at hand.
- Unfavorable environmental condition under which the task must be performed.
- Inadequate tools and resources required to perform the task.
- Limited time allocated for the performance of the task.
- Inadequate preparation for the task in question.
- Fear and other emotional factors

Helping the child to overcome his/her weakness

A parent is obliged to put structures in place to ensure that growing children is able to make strength out of their weaknesses. Below are suggested strategies that can be employed by the parent to realize this.

- Giving the necessary training to the child
- Motivating the child
- Providing the necessary resources required for optimal growth
- Give reasonable time limit for the performance of an activity
- Providing answers to the child's questions to clear all doubt.

CHAPTER SIX

39

THE SECRETS OF YOUR CHILD

Secrets are pieces of information concerning events; happenings; instances that people prefer to keep them away from public knowledge. As humanity's existence revolves around happenings, secrets shall continue to be a part of our life. Same applies to children. Depending on type of parent a child has, many could be the secrets to be kept from both parties.

Reasons for keeping secrets

- To avoid unnecessary involvement by certain groups of people you consider external
- To prevent disgrace
- To avoid trouble
- To protect the dignity of their personality
- To have enough privacy to bond with those who have been chosen.

Secrets a child might keep from the parents

As already stated, the degree of secrecy of a child with respects to parents is dependent on the type of parenting style used by the parents.

- The child's boyfriend or girlfriend
- The child's sex life
- Damaged things
- Scores in tests
- Associations joined
- Running from school.
- Involvement with drugs
- Unhealthy company
- School issues particularly learning difficulties.

CHAPTER SEVEN

THE DREAMS OF YOUR CHILD

In one breadth, dreams can be explained as a series of images, concepts, feelings, and experiences that frequently happen uncontrollably in the mind during particular phases of sleep. in another context dream represent mental, abstract and hopeful pictures of future aspirations that individuals hold and intend to work towards achieving in the nearest possible time.

For the purpose of our discussion the latter definition of dream shall be used. As progressive humans, we always seek to better ourselves in life. Every person including children have wild dreams of what they intend to achieve in the near future. When asked what they (children) to be in future: children shall bring out several interesting revelations of how they want to shape their future.

Things that influence child's dreams.

Personal and career dreams child make up are influenced by several factors: among them are the following;

- The home setting of the child. This refers to how things are put in the place in the child's immediate family. It talks about the family's perception about life success, beliefs and general aspirations. The family history also comes to play.
- The school setting of the child. This revolves around the kind of knowledge learners are given in the school. The type of practical examples alluded to in the school coupled with the type of school system a child finds himself. The type of school system employed determines the types students that are produced. Thus, an effective and vibrant school system is very much likely to produce useful students who can contribute to the development of the country as a whole.
- The community setting. This describes the type of community the child hails from, stays and schools. The community the child finds himself/herself determines what the child sees which culminates to what the child wishes to be. The child's dream is influenced by what s/he sees, hears and interacts with in the community. The adult generation serve as a reference for the younger ones. The more sophisticated the adult population are: the more sophisticated the younger population shall be. This is in view of the fact that, the adult serves as the point of reference for the younger.

In sum, what a child dream of becoming is influenced by what he usually sees, hear and interact with.

How to shape/realize the dream of a child

- Provide the best form of education
- Provide and exemplary setting in the home
- Offer the child the counselling about future prospects
- Show interest in the life of the child by having intermittent interactive sessions with the child
- Make the necessary provision for the optimal growth of the child.

CHAPTER EIGHT

THE PERSONALITY OF YOUR CHILD

The personality a child grows with goes a long way to determine the general perception about. It influences how a child sees his or her future

The concept of personality

Personality is a distinctive style of feeling, thinking, and acting. In interactions with other individuals, personality is most obviously portrayed and include moods, attitudes, and opinions. It entails behavioral traits that set one person apart from another and that may be seen in how people interact with their surroundings and their social groups.

A person's distinct thought, mood, and behavior patterns that set them apart from others are referred to as their personality. The influence of biological and environmental factors on personality is constant throughout life. Our traits types, temperaments, and character are just a few examples of how personality can be represented in various ways. The way we connect with others and react to situations is also influenced by our personalities.

Things that make up the personality of a child.

- How you address people.
- How you dress up
- Your reaction to issues
- Your beliefs and inputs about issues
- Your choices during decision making.

Contributing to your child's personality formation.

Self-awareness is the first step in developing your personality. Assess your child's qualities and areas that need improvement. The development of your child's personality borders around but not limited to the following;

- *Know the traits of your child.* Thus, making a list of peculiar actions, inactions and reactions that characterize your child shall paint a clear picture about the general personality of your child.
- *Sort the enlisted traits into constructive and destructive:* This will enable the parent to identify which of the traits needs to be upheld for the overall development of the child. This act shall also bring to light the traits that need to be halted or minimized.
- *Assess how you can improve on the destructive traits and catalyze the progress of the constructive.*

REFERENCES

Understanding Sexual Behaviour in Children | NSPCC[1]

What is sex? - Women's Health Matters (womenshealthmatters.org.au)[2]

4 Ways to Develop Personality - wikiHow[3]

https://www.wikihow.com/Identify-Your-Strengths

https://www.choosingwisdom.org/7-ways-discover-your-strengths-how-use/

https://www.bing.com/search?q=what+are+professional+strengths&qs=n&form=QBRE&sp=-1

https://positivepsychology.com/what-are-your-strengths/

https://positivepsychology.com/what-are-your-strengths/

https://www.purelovequotes.com/images/quotes/900/the-greatest-pleasure-in-life-is-love-euripides.jpg?v=1

https://psychcentral.com/relationships/the-psychology-of-love

https://www.verywellmind.com/what-is-love-2795343#Is%20Love%20Influenced%20by%20Biology%20O[4]?

https://www.nspcc.org.uk/keeping-children-safe/sex-relationships/sexual-behaviour-children/

https://www.womenshealthmatters.org.au/womens-health-wellbeing/sexual-and-reproductive-health/all-about-sex/what-is-sex/

1. https://www.nspcc.org.uk/keeping-children-safe/sex-relationships/sexual-behaviour-children/

2. https://www.womenshealthmatters.org.au/womens-health-wellbeing/sexual-and-reproductive-health/all-about-sex/what-is-sex/

3. https://www.wikihow.com/Develop-Personality

4. https://www.verywellmind.com/what-is-love-2795343#Is_0bcef9c45bd8a48eda1b26eb0c61c869_20Love_0bcef9c45bd8a48eda1b26eb0c61c869_20Influenced_0bcef9c45bd8a48eda1b26eb0c61c869_20by_0bcef9c45bd8a48eda1b26eb0c61c869_20Biology_0bcef9c45bd8a48eda1b26eb0c61c869_20Or_0bcef9c45bd8a48eda1b26eb0c61c869_20Culture

https://cihr-irsc.gc.ca/e/48642.html

Don't miss out!

Visit the website below and you can sign up to receive emails whenever LUKE MENSAH AKROSUMA publishes a new book. There's no charge and no obligation.

https://books2read.com/r/B-A-NVCZ-JOWKC

BOOKS 2 READ

Connecting independent readers to independent writers.

About the Author

He hails from Tainso in the Bono region. His basic education was completed at University Junior High School, Cape Coast. Then proceeded to Sunyani Senior High School for Senior High School.

His academic exploits are evident in his academic achievement by obtaining First Class Honors in Diploma in Basic Education and First Class Honors in Bachelor of Education Mathematics both at the University of Cape Coast, Ghana.

He is currently married with a daughter.